Phenomenology of Tools

Philosophical Observations on the Nature of Tool Wielding

Also included

On the Marriage of Tools, Art, and History:
Curator's Riff

H. G. Brack

Copyright © 2010 by Harold Brack

ISBN 13 978-0-9829951-0-5

First published in July 1982 by Pennywheel Press, West Jonesport, Maine

Cover design by Sett Balise featuring Alan Magee's *Tryptic: Thingpoem, Inheritance, Helix.* (For more information see Appendix B.)

On the Marriage of Tools, Art, and History: Curator's Riff, first published in 2005 in *What Needs to Be Retrieved: The Marriage of Tools, Art and History* by The Davistown Museum, art show catalog June 25, 2005 through October 10, 2005.

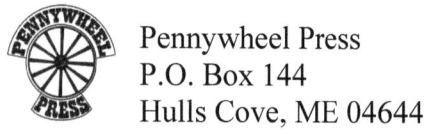

Pennywheel Press
P.O. Box 144
Hulls Cove, ME 04644

Acknowledgements

I wish to acknowledge my indebtedness to Martin Heidegger, whose innovative use of language in *Being and Time* (1926) was a seminal event in philosophy and an inspiration for this undertaking. I wish also to acknowledge Suzanne Langer, Jane Ellen Harrison, Thomas Kuhn, Erwin Panofsky, John Gofman, R. W. Riseborough and others who inadvertently contributed to this book.

H. G. Brack
West Jonesport, ME
May 12, 1982

Acknowledgements for the Second Edition

Many thanks, to Beth Sundberg, Sett Balise, and Judith Bradshaw Brown for their assistance.

Table of Contents

Preface to the Second Edition iii
The Phenomenology of Tools 1
On the Marriage of Tools, Art, and History: Curator's Riff 73
Appendix A: Eaton's Boatyard 83
Appendix B: Notes and Commentary on the Illustrations 85
Appendix C: Pennywheel Press Publications 93

Preface to the Second Edition

The *Phenomenology of Tools* was written in the 1970s at locations such as the Clapp Library at Wellesley College (MA) and the University of London. Abstracted to the brief text which follows, it was published in 1982 in the context of the evolution of a thriving tool salvage business, which focused on the recovery and recycling of the hand tools that are the legacy of New England's maritime and industrial heritage, an ongoing endeavor not obviously related to the philosophical content of this text.

Four decades have passed since the first tool store opened its doors in West Jonesport, Maine, in 1970. Some of the forge-welded, signed edge tools and other artifacts recovered since then now reside in the collections of the Davistown Museum, established in 1999. In 2005, the museum exhibited its permanent collection of edge tools and art as a component of the show *What Needs to Be Retrieved: The Marriage of Tools, Art, and History*. The introductory essay in the show catalog is reproduced in the second section of this edition of the *Phenomenology of Tools*. It provides a less abstract synopsis of the phenomenology of tools, especially as experienced and presented by New England artists, toolmakers, and others in the permanent collection of the museum.

Using a poem by Philip Booth (*Appendix A*) as a context in which to explore the show's theme of the marriage of tools, art, and history, both the "Curator's Riff" and the exhibition explore a key element of the phenomenology of tools that is only briefly referenced in the first edition text, i.e. the pleasures of the convivial use of tools. From the simple joys of gardening to the subtle satisfaction of mechanics, machinists, artisans, and artists, an enduring lesson of forty years as a "mooncusser" (tool salvaging) is how much fun we have with our tools. Decades of observing the enjoyment that both tool customers and museum visitors express upon buying, owning, using, or viewing tools stand in contrast to the round-world disconnectedness of information age electronic technology.

As the urban, suburban, and rural archaeological excavations of the Jonesport Wood Company's search for old woodworking tools evolved and the Liberty Tool Company opened in 1976, working artisans and artists found the two tool stores to be sources for tools used in home workshops and for the repair and construction of equipment and buildings of every description. Artists used many of these tools to create art in a wide variety of media. After 1976 and the opening of the Liberty Tool Co., tools were often traded for art. David McLaughlin's *Study for Welds* (Figure 25) was the first such work obtained in trade for tools. This acquisition marks the first stage in the evolution of the art collected at the Davistown Museum, a selection of which is illustrated in this edition.

Closely connected with the 1982 publication of the *Phenomenology of Tools* was the ongoing collection of the artifacts and information that led to the establishment of the Davistown Museum and its publication series *Hand Tools in History*. The tools and technologies discussed in these essays were the lynchpins of the florescence of an American industrial society now being eclipsed by the mass produced consumer goods of developing nations such as China and South Korea. One volume in this series, *Registry of Maine Toolmakers* is now in its sixth edition and is a testament to the skills and tenacity of the obscure shipsmiths and toolmakers working in Maine. The other volumes explore the history of steel edge tool fabrication and the production and use of such tools in maritime and industrial New England.

Appendix C presents a listing of Pennywheel Press publications, including the *Hand Tools in History* publications, which celebrate the creative accomplishments of American toolmakers. *Appendix B* provides background information and commentary about the art in the permanent collection of the Davistown Museum illustrated in this edition. These works of art embody the marriage of tools, art, and history, an essential component of the philosophical peregrinations of the *Phenomenology of Tools*.

Frequently referenced in the *Phenomenology of Tools* is the perplexing irony of what we do with our tools. The follow-up to the *Hand Tools in History* series, the *Phenomenology of Biocatastrophe* explores the specific environmental, technological, scientific, historical, and social constituents of the mad rush of global military/industrial/consumer society to self-annihilation. The tendency of human society to utilize tools for destructive purposes began with weapons production and now extends to the unintended external costs of petrochemistry, information age electronic detritus, consumer-product-derived environmental chemicals, and a predatory shadow banking network. The evolution and unabated growth of a global consumer society has distinct world commons limits that provide a sobering context for our celebration of the conviviality of tools. What would the inventive toolmakers of the florescence of America's maritime and industrial milieu, the creators of the tools that built a nation, think if they could apprehend the biogeochemical nightmares that we have created with our information age marriage of technology, greed, and history? This technological and social apostasy stands in contrast to the creative use of tools explored in "Curator's Riff" and expressed by the artists in the museum collection.

Modern global consumer society is not shy about celebrating the many benefits accrued by flat world electronic technologies, biopharmaceutical and genomic wizards, and an industrial agricultural system that could feed ten billion world citizens assuming they, or benevolent governments and/or NGOs, have the money to pay for post-peak oil transportation and production costs. The growing world water crisis and the accelerating contamination of human serum, lipids, breast milk, and maternal cord blood with endocrine disrupting chemicals and many other ecotoxins are unfortunate consequences of a growing world population and the evolution of a consumer society where the phenomenology of tools includes more than the convivial edge tools produced by New England's shipsmiths and toolmakers. The growing dead zones, wastelands, resource depletion, and world indebtedness are signals of the beginning of the age of biocatastrophe. This is the downside of the phenomenology of tools, often referenced in the text that follows and explored in detail in the final volumes of the Davistown Museum's publications about the biohistory of industrial technology.

With the end of the Cold War and the lessening of the threat of nuclear annihilation, an apocalyptic ending to human civilization may be a less likely outcome than the gradual implosion of global consumer society due to the collapse of ecosystem diversity and productivity, chemical fallout, a lack of potable water, and growing individual, governmental, and market economy world debt. Biocatastrophe, the inevitable result of the misuse of our tools and technologies, is the defining historical event of the 21st century. Not to document and debate this seminal event in human history is to deceive ourselves about the inevitable fate of the world commons. The ongoing mass media rituals of aversion about the inevitability of biocatastrophe constitute an evasion of the most important component of the phenomenology of tools: what we do with our tools and the legacy we are leaving for future generations.

Dasein may be an unfamiliar term. Translated from the German, Dasein does not "mean," but "is" the existential experience of being in the world:

>Dasein laughs, loves, touches Spirit,
>Uncovers joy, listens to Conscience.
>Steadfastness, Care, Solicitude…
>
>Love is the Dancing of Dasein
>On the horizon of death; (pg. 59)

The Phenomenology of Tools

Figure 1. Carol Hanson, *Yemaya*, Davistown Museum Hulls Cove Sculpture Garden.

Figure 2. Sett Balise, *Main Hall,* Davistown Museum, Liberty, Maine.

I.

Dasein, thrown in Time,
    Androgynous imagist,
        Manipulator of found nature,
      Inscriber of symbol in icon and ground,
        Discursive designer of science,
    Inadvertent inventor of art.

Figure 3. Collection of shells and beads in a dish, Davistown Museum, Main Hall, Case B.

Dasein, tool maker and tool wielder,
    Creative Kourous,
    Orphic artisan,
    Cultural cartographer,
    Sign maker and energetic aphorist
    Gives an inexorable voice
        To the summoning of history.

Figure 4. Birmingham smooth plane, Main Hall, Case K.

Dasein, subliminal symbolist,
    Writes history with factical tools.
Inscribing implements, icons of history,
    Manifest the metaphysical
        In a phenomenology of the technical.
A silent soliloquy beckons
    To inquisitive Dasein.

Figure 5. Toby Stewart, *Patina*, Davistown Museum Maine Artists Guild, Room 3.

History is not unilinear,
    But simultaneous fields
        Of tool wielders in time and space.
Dasein historicizes with ontical
    And ontological tools;
        Unintended images uncover history.

Figure 6. David McLaughlin, *Used Glove Salesperson's Bicycle: Post Apocalypse Series Number 3*, Main Hall.

Evolution is Dasein equipping itself;
    The human brain,
        Instrument of operations
     Surrounded by found resources,
        Wields nature as tool creating more
          tools.
Ideology is an eleventh hour invention,
      Instrument of ominous apostasy.

Figure 7. Wampum, Main Hall, Case C.

Dasein signs Time silently;
    Forms of tools, patterns of culture.
Hidden voices outstripping Time
    Recollect the hubbub of history.
Transuranic alpha wielding Dasein
    Creates a new historical era;
        Unseen ionizing inhalations
    Omen of apocalypse in a horizon of
        entropy.

Figure 8. Moose hide scraper, Main Hall, Case B.

II.

The archaeology of tools
    Presents found object as primal tool.
A million years of eoliths
    Preceded the first knappered axe.
A lithic litany
    Of conchoidal siliceous fractures
        Discloses Dasein appropriating nature.

Figure 9. Rattle, Main Hall, Case C.

Eolith became coup-de-poing;
    The historizing of tools began.
Cryptographic stone tools,
    Fire pits, kitchen middens,
Severe cold, cave as shelter-tool.
Cave drawings the mimetic mark
    Of Dasein re-presenting imagination

Figure 10. Apache mortar and pestle, Main Hall.

PaleoDasein wielded found resources,
    Will to power over nature.
Pottery, weaving, husbandry,
    The ground stone axe,
        The Natufian assemblage:
    Images of the incipient Neolithic revolution.
Prehistoric Dasein lived in nature;
    Historic Dasein lives beside nature.

Figure 11. Monte Alban funerary vase, Main Hall, Case A.

Chthonic ritual, optimistic animism,
    Totem, taboo, cornucopia.
Purification, consecration, initiation,
    Rites of sacrifice
        Evolved into rituals of tendance.
The hymn of the Kouretes
    Became the myth of an anthropo-
        morphic Zeus.

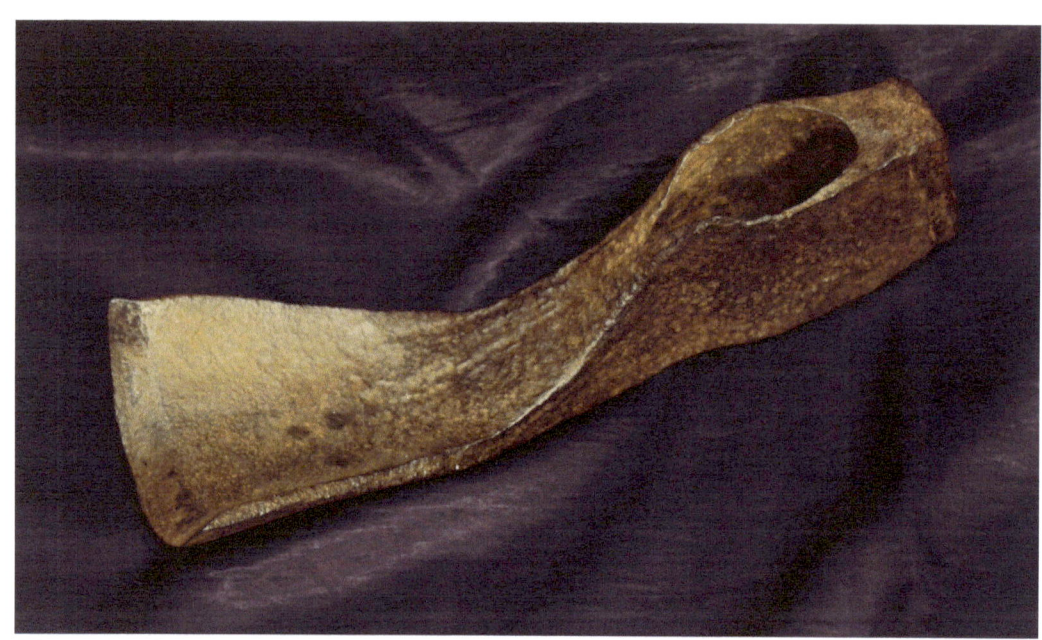
Figure 12. Gutter adz, Art of the Edge Tool Exhibition, Main Hall.

Bronze sword, tool of conquest,
    Plow and irrigation,
        Instruments of food surplus.
Slavery, writing, bureaucracy,
    Hierarchy of civilization.
Heuristic Dasein discovered metallurgy,
    Scientific magic.

Figure 13. Unknown artist, *Medieval City with Serfs*, Room T, Print Department.

Voice-directed bicameral Dasein
    Fell out of nature
        Into platonic idealism.
Dasein traded taboo
    For Eleusinian mystery;
The magical manipulation of nature
    Became the incipient oracle of
        empiricism.

Figure 14. Kilroy, *Earth Reliquary*, Main Hall.

Myth of Atlantis, battle of Troy,
    Lost and Found history
        Uncovers Dasein always aggrandizing.
Iron tools, steel swords,
    Revolutionary smelting.
Empire, conquest, slavery,
    Reappearing images of violence.

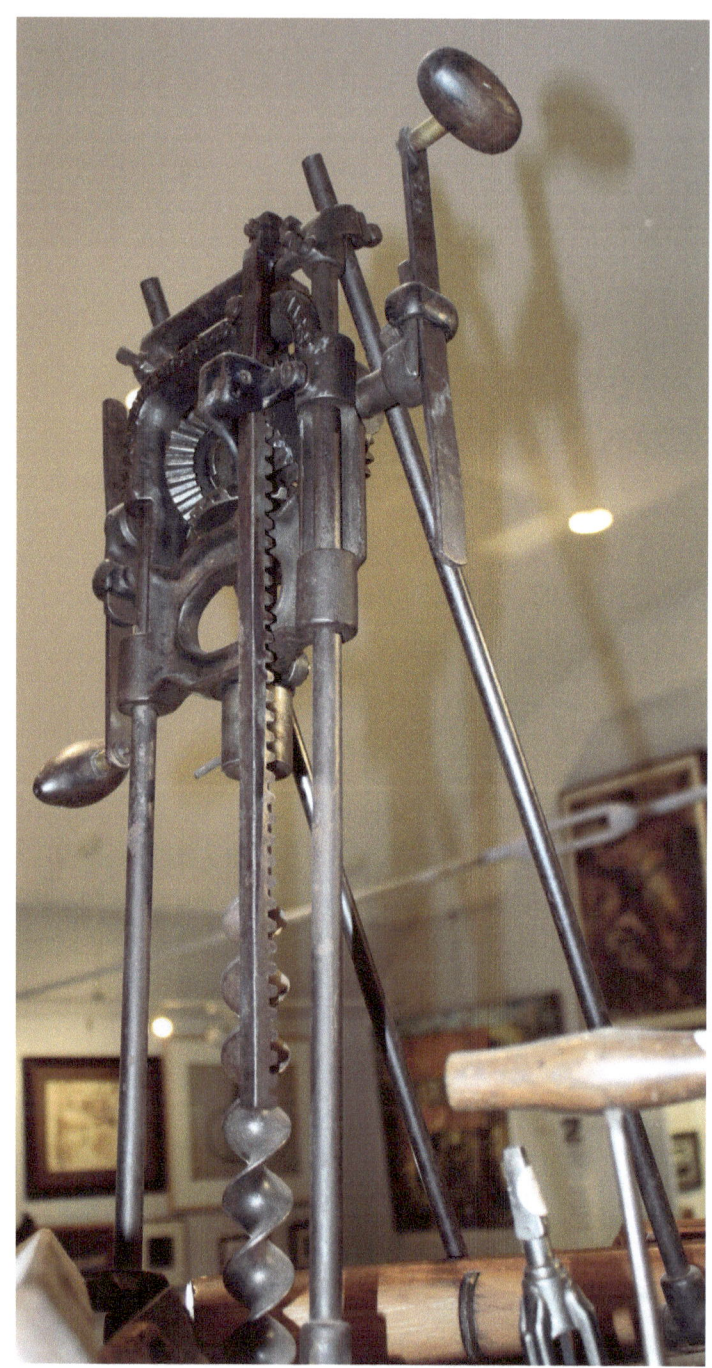

Figure 15. Millers Falls mortising drill, Main Hall.

Celtiberic and Gaelic sailors
    Left inscrutable runic marks
        In sleepy Vitramannaland.
Ship's compass, gunpowder,
    Revolution with a printing press.
Bedazzled Renaissance Dasein wielded illusions
    Of an ideal order of nature.

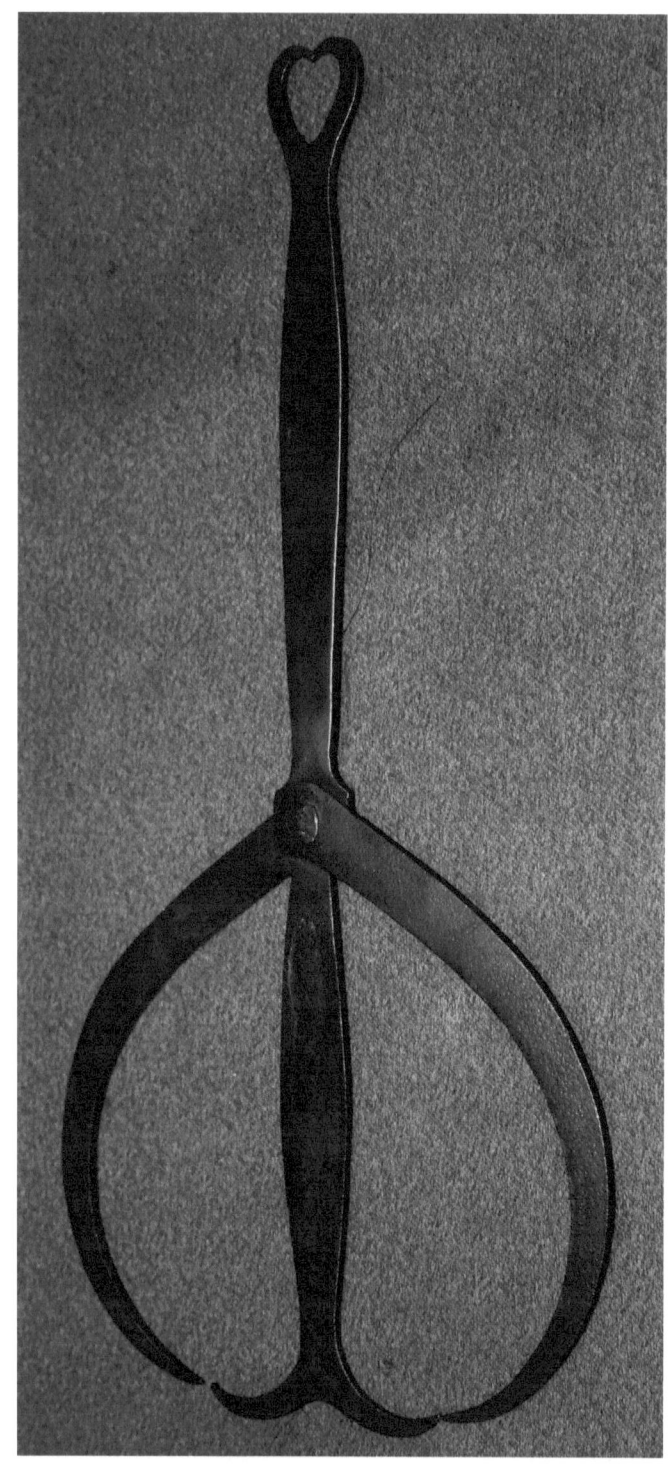

Figure 16. Blacksmith double calipers, Main Hall.

Cooper, Sawyer, Blacksmith, Tinsmith
   Welded hand-made hand tools,
     Conventional, essential,
       Everyday equipment,
  Metaphors of craftsmanship,
    Icons of Freedom and Unfreedom
Inundated by the cacophony
   of technology.

Figure 17. Nate Nichols, *Bike with Riders*, Main Hall.

The Industrial Revolution
    Was that widening gyre
        Of one technology begetting another.
Myth lost ritual, gained method;
    Technique as totem,
        Nature a concept of power.
The new economic serfdom of Dasein
    Premonition of a final conquest of nature.

Figure 18. Buff and Buff surveying transit, Main Hall.

American individualist
    Consumes resource as birthright.
        Competition is a ritual,
            Expertise as Initiation.
Growth is a sacrament;
    Wealth is lumber, coal, oil, gold.
Narcissistic Dasein dissipates
    Biosphere as bank account.

Figure 19. Phil Barter, *Gas Tank*, Main Hall.

Oil as tool is found biomass;
    Car as tool drives Dasein.
Inner directed industrial Dasein
    Is short-circuited by electronic anxiety.
Telescoping technology disconnects
    Generation from generation;
        New energy idioms
    Dissociate Dasein from nature.

Figure 20. Buddy Swenson, *American Portrait #6: In a Time of War*, Davistown Museum Maine Artists Guild, Main Hall.

The language of electronic music
    Reconnects irrational Dasein
        To primordial melodies.
Other electronic equipment,
    Instruments of propaganda or warfare,
        Distract Dasein from Freedom.

Figure 21. H. G. Brack, *Mixed Grill Number 4: Anthropogenic Radioactivity*, Main Hall.

Proliferating inventions of destruction
    Undermine a fragile ecological existence.
Paradoxical paradigms, elite illusions,
    Atomic cybernetic alienation.
Ahistorical post-industrial Dasein
    Lingers on the edge of biocatastrophe.

Figure 22. Lauren Fensterstock, *Cheeseburger w/ Sesame Seeds and Accidental Durable Remnants*, Main Hall.

Water is tool for biosphere,
    Instrument of life,
        Ground of protoplasm.
Scurrying Dasein concocts a new primal soup:
    Maleficent mixture of dioxin,
        Methylmercury, persistent pesticides;
    Radioactive water cycle.

Figure 23. Davis level, Main Hall.

The technological elite
   race forward;
Second comers slouch towards obsolescence.
A hungry third world
   Is mired in antique expectations.
The death of Nature
   Is in all ways rationalized.
              * * * *

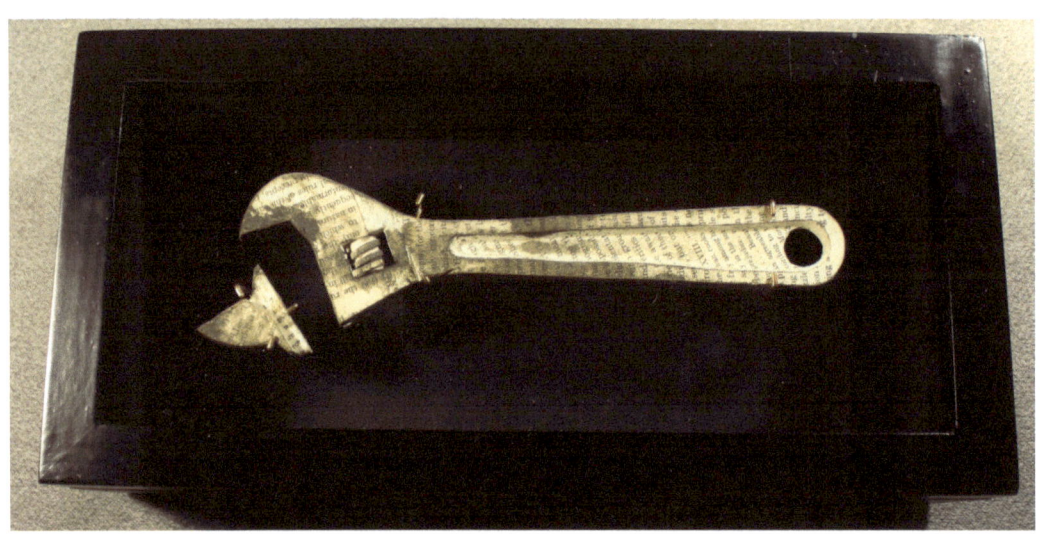

Figure 24. Aaron Stephan, *Wrench*, Main Hall.

III

Discursive Dasein wields ideology
    Religion, philosophy,
        The transcendental equipment
           Of civilized Dasein.
Symboling Dasein brandishes tongue
    Tooled by syntax, vocabulary, dictionary.
Dasein historizes ethos and ethics
    With the speech of his tools.

Figure 25. David McLaughlin, *Study for Welds*, Davistown Museum Hulls Cove Sculpture Garden.

Art the speech of Dasein in non-words;
    Rhythm, harmony, melody,
        The discourse of music.
Petroglyph, hieroglyph, cuneiform,
    Language tools antecedent to alphabet.
Now Dasein wields a silicon speech
    And chooses convivial stratagems
        Or Scientific Sophistry.

Figure 26. J. Wood, *Box Scraper under Glass*, Main Hall.

Visual Art discloses the intrinsic
    In an iconography of image
        Or non-image.
Lost Art is intended, ignored, rediscovered.
Found Art is unintended, untended,
    An inadvertent incantation
        Outside of Time.

Figure 27. Obadiah Buell, *Arch (reliquary for carriage-maker's plane)*, Main Hall.

The discursive symbolism of science
   Is an insufficient language
      For the Speech of Care.
Neither Hope nor Love are verifiable,
   But have existence and efficacy
      And present themselves in silence.

Figure 28. Melita Westerlund, *Balancing Act*, Main Hall.

Hebraic Dasein expressed the value of Care
    In the concept of law.
Blind faith is a dogma,
    Leap of faith an epiphany.
Spirit is disclosed, not conceived.
Let the death of God
    Be the death of pure reason.

Figure 29. H. G. Brack, *Socratic Dog*, Main Hall.

Father, Son and Holy Ghost
    Are coeval with Lucifer and Beelzebub.
Heaven and Hell are equiprimordial;
    Purgatory is Now.
Beware the illusion of Christological Innocence,
    Paradise later
        May be abnormally radioactive.

Figure 30. George Daniell, *Georgia O'Keefe at Her Home in NM*, Main Hall.

Dasein laughs, loves, touches Spirit,
    Uncovers joy, listens to Conscience.
        Steadfastness, Care, Solicitude
    The ultimate ontological tools
        For compassionate Dasein.
Love is the Dancing of Dasein
    On the horizon of death;
        The Suchness of Dance
    Is a Touching beyond factical touch.

Figure 31. Dan Falt, *Attack Rabbit*, Davistown Museum Maine Artists Guild, Room 5.

IV

Zoomorphic Dasein found tools in nature,
    Prophetic discovery,
        Ground of culture.
Anthropocentric Dasein wields tools
    Against nature.
The Calling of Dasein
    Began with invocation
        And shall perish in a rite of
            burnt sacrifice.

Figure 32. Squidge Davis, *Night Holding the Moon*, Main Hall.

Dasein-in-nullity externalizes,
    Confiscates, exterminates nature;
        Illusion of the ascent of man.
The primordial fear of infertility,
    Cold, hunger, darkness,
        Is the vestigial origin
    For the contempt of nature.

Figure 33. Lewis Iselin, *Agony*, Davistown Museum Hulls Cove Sculpture Garden.

Anomalous technology, ironic predicament,
    Dasein is fallen into duplicity.
The predominant images of tools in history:
    Forgotten brutality, cruelty, barbarism;
        Benevolent science subsumed by
            violence.
Optimistic ahistorical Dasein
    Conquers nature in a dance of death.

Figure 34. Don (Brother Hugh) Vanesse, *Massachusetts Prisons 200 Years Later*, Stairwell Entrance to Main Hall.

The perfection of method
    And the cult of profit
        Conceals the phenomenology of tools
    From unphilosophic Dasein.
Unsuspecting Dasein etches tell-tale images
    As misunderstood history;
        Unwise wielding is the doom of
            Dasein.

Figure 35. H. G. Brack, *Three Wise Men and Baby Jesus*, Davistown Museum Hulls Cove Sculpture Garden.

Cue of Quantum Mechanics,
    Theory of Elementary Catastrophes.
Acid rain, radioactive snow,
    Chlorinated hydrocarbons
        In marine ecosystems.
Strontium 90, cesium 137,
    Plutonium radionuclides:
Listen to the speech of nuclear tools,
    Inescapable image of biocide.

Figure 36. Unknown artist, *St. Francis*, Davistown Museum Hulls Cove Sculpture Garden.

Transcend the apparition of power,
    Stretch the conception of technology;
       Include convivial science,
          Ecological ethics,
      Exorcise the nuclear image.
        Reform our repertoire of tools -
Or destroy with our creativity
    The Ground of our Being.

On the Marriage of Tools, Art, and History: Curator's Riff
by H. G. Skip Brack

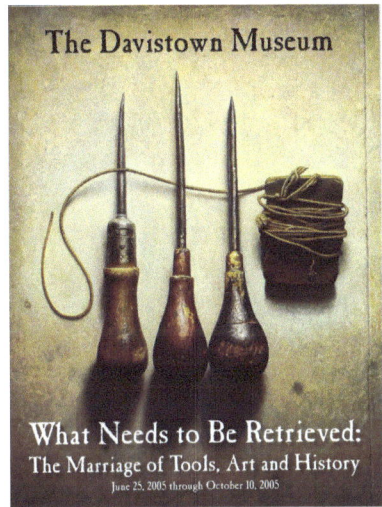

Figure 37. Art catalog cover.

The 2005 Davistown Museum exhibition, "What Needs to Be Retrieved: The Marriage of Tools, Art, and History," offers an opportunity to revisit the museum's mission of collecting and interpreting the hand tools of New England's maritime culture and juxtaposing them with the work of contemporary Maine artists. It presents sculpture, paintings, drawings, prints, and other works that incorporate tools and related found objects as part of their imagery. The show also highlights a selection of tools from the museum's permanent collection, illustrating the historical and metallurgical issues, on which we focus our on-going documentation.

It is our intention that the art featuring images of tools or incorporating them juxtaposed with the tools themselves encourage viewers to explore the interrelationships between tools, art, and history. It offers a journey into the language of tools, beginning with the simplicity of the everyday use of hand tools and the beauty of handmade hand tools. Exploring the relationship of tools to history, as well as tools as art objects, is the central mission of the museum and forms a cornerstone of this exhibition.

More debatable and difficult to articulate are the many and diverse ways in which individual artists relate to, experience, or incorporate tools in their art. The art in the show ranges from traditional narration to iconography of near magical luminescence, from classical compositions of welded steel, polychromed or not, and photography to assemblages of found artifacts and abstract conceptual sculpture. Words become inadequate for describing the aesthetic resonance and historical story-telling of the artworks on display. We hope that this exhibition will take visitors on a journey beyond the rich legacy of the toolmakers of New England's maritime and industrial past to experience the links between art, artifact, history, and the iconography of tools, a journey on which the written word may no longer be the vehicle.

Pleasures of the Text I

Lay out the hand tools in any tool chest or workshop, and you have a text. What is your pleasure in how you read this text?

Figure 38. Roger Majorowicz, *Kings Mill II*.

Are these tools functional objects for everyday use, to be taken up again and put back to work – the wood chisel of the boatwright, the socket wrench of the mechanic, the wrecking bar to take down the old woodshed, the mattock for the garden, the machinist's caliper recycled by a jeweler or guitar maker?

Or, are these tools going to be set aside, not used again. Are they orphaned objects, no longer functional? Will they be forgotten, then lost? If they will not be retrieved again as useful objects, is there some other way their presence and their heritage will speak to us again?

The phenomenology of tools is the way tools help us construct the world around us, our perceptual milieu where the language of tools speaks to us in a diversity of ways beyond their role as simple, functioning objects. This discussion of the marriage of tools, art, and history explores the interrelationships between simple craftsmanship of tool users and makers and the iconography of the artisans and artists who use tools to make history and art.

This marriage can be irritating, uncomfortable, even unfathomable for craftspersons and artists who just want to use tools, "make do, making a living, throw nothing away." So then, should we turn away from exploring the

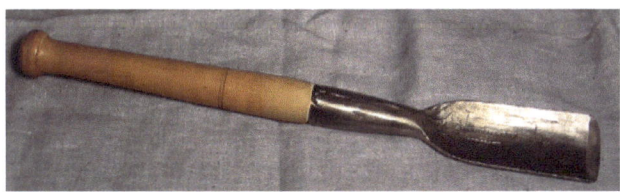

Figure 39. Libby and Bolton gouge, Portland, ME, c. 1857-1886.

significance of tools as cultural artifacts? Why not take up the "requisite" tool and explore "the idea" it begins to shape up? To open ourselves to the many voices of tools is to travel from the above-ground simplicity of function and technical skill into an Alice rabbit hole and the underground labyrinth of tools in history, each room telling a different story of how tools were used, the society they built, the ecosystems they altered, and the images they created.

Pleasures of the Text II

A fundamental pleasure of hand tools, beyond the simplicity of everyday use, lies in the artisans' pride in craft. Implicit in the drawshave buried in pot warp is the confidence of technique; its effective use depends upon the marriage of skill and intuition. The history of any trade –shipwright, blacksmith, stone mason, machinist, tinsmith, jeweler, watchmaker – includes the legacy of skills and knowledge passed from one generation to another. Much of this knowledge is scientific, the discursive description of woodworking skills and equipment, for example the forging, quenching, and tempering of edge tools; stone cutting techniques; milling machine calibration and operation; the use of the combination square; or the microstructure of steel in the watch spring.

Figure 40. Cheese whisk, c. 1800.

But much of the craft knowledge passed from generation to generation is also intuitive, a feeling for how to do things correctly. The blacksmith's knowledge of texture, color, fracture; the wooden boat builder's of mortising or joinery; the stone cutter's finesse; the tool designer's genius all express the relationship of feeling to form. The success of the art of the toolmaker, the artist using tools to make art, or the evocative images of tools in art is contingent upon the opportune union of technique and inspiration. Whole civilizations have succeeded or failed because of the marriage or divorce of skill and intuition.

Tools Write History

Hand tools write history, building ideas into artifact. The history of how the adz was made recapitulates the metallurgical innovations in the formation of civilizations. Lever, wheel and axle, pulley, inclined plane, wedge, and screw are the simple machines that were and are everyday instruments of construction and repair. Wooden ships were axed, sawed, adzed, bored, shaped, trunneled, caulked, roped, and rigged into a historical reality that is the marriage of history and the art of the shipwright.

Hand tools transformed ideas and ideology into social and industrial history. Bog iron hammer. Wrought iron blacksmith tongs. Forged steel hewing ax. Crucible steel framing chisel. Coasting schooner. The first milling machine. Brownstone cityscapes. The electric power grid. And now, tools build machines that make other machines, making handmade tools obsolete.

Figure 41. Patent model of a brick-making machine, c. 1878.

But not quite. Ancient and contemporary crafts and trades have an ironic relevance in the age of the Internet. Our electronic interconnectedness propagates memories of the rhythm of convivial hand tools hammering, filing, and sawing reality into little pieces of history we can savor, if we take the time to listen. Will our awareness of the interrelationship of tools and history help us make do in a post-industrial age of electronic anxiety, where the skills and traditions of the arts and crafts of the past may be essential to family and community survival in the future?

Archaeology of Tools

Tools no longer used become orphaned objects, laid down, not to be retrieved as functioning instruments. These are accidental durable remnants, set aside, then lost and buried layer upon layer in palimpsests waiting for archaeologists and historians to peel them back and reveal the stories of history. Fluted, bifurcated, then notched points. Ground stone and bone tools. Pottery chards. Wampum drilled with iron bits. The archaeology of tools unmasks prehistory, protohistory, and then history itself. Bog iron – natural steel. Blast furnace – German steel. Cementation furnace – Blister steel. Puddling furnace – crucible steel. Orphan tools linger, uncovering the stories of history – the steam engine, the factory system, the internal combustion engine.

Then unpleasant questions arise. What have we done with our tools? What kind of society have we built? What labyrinths await our peripatetic children? Chlorinated hydrocarbons in cheeseburgers. The age of anthropogenic radioactivity. The archaeology of tools begins with eoliths and ends with unwanted traces of technology in our shrinking small planet diet. The Industrial Revolution has come and gone. What stories does the material cultural legacy of tools tell us in the age of electromagnetic transmutations and ubiquitous chemical fallout?

The Art of the Toolmaker

Figure 42. C. Gove plow plane, Kittery, ME, c. 1840.

Toolmaking, like tool wielding and the image making of artists with tools, is an art itself. Many have forgotten the art of the toolmaker, the tools themselves subsumed in the history they created. Only a few of the tools that make history and art disclose themselves as art itself – a wrought iron cheese whip, a wantage rule, a hay thief, a paneling plane. The first augers were handmade, not drop-forged. The laborious forging of natural steel produced one tool at a time, an individual act of consecration, every tool a part of the text of his/her story.

Hammer on anvil. Temper. Quench. Anneal. The shaping of the idea of the ductile durable edge tool. Old hand tools have a way of transforming themselves into sculpture in time, the tool itself as orphaned art. Which tools will reveal themselves as icons in some future peeling back of the palimpsests of history?

Artists and Their Tools

Figure 43. Wantage rule, c. 1720.

The craftsperson uses tools to make history; artists use tools to make art. Art is image that is painted, etched, hammered, filed, fired, forged, scribbled, flung, quenched, photographed, and then measured and sliced into increments of reality that celebrate the creativity of the artist as tool user. The quiet solitude of the artist's workshop is a sacred and private space. Carving tools and mallet. Dapping block and burin. Palette and brush. Hammer and anvil. Pen and ink. Bench plate and stake. Tongs and nozzle. Artists use tools to make art that marries the simplicity of function with the finesse of creativity to give birth to images which tell stories without words. The writing of the text with color, line, volume, space, movement. Form as the conception of surfaces – transparent, translucent, opaque. The transmigration of artifact into art. The impasto of composition transmutes artifact into art.

Artists create new icons or reconstruct old images in ways that expand how we see, feel, and listen, transporting us by epiphany to places we have never been, altering our being in the world.

Images of Tools in Art

The transition from cultural artifact and images made by the tool itself to the image of tools in art or as art object involves a journey from everyday instruments of representation and narration to a magical evocation of tools as icons in compositions that form the interface of memory, history, technique, and the sublime. New texts created from rediscovered orphan objects. Remembered rhythms of tools of the past – hand plane, saw set, paintbrush. The memento mori, the subtle humor of the trompe l'oeil, the search for the continuity between the past and present. Ancient icons inscribed on canvas or thrust in space, recapitulating the memory of simple acts.

Sculptors, painters, etchers, engravers, ironmongers, and assemblage artists weave mundane found artifacts into a chorus of sculpture objects and still lifes, lingering images that enliven how today feels, reconnecting what needs to be retrieved in a marriage of function, form, and storytelling.

The Invisibility of Tools in Art

Figure 44. Melita Westerlund, *Magician's Dream*.

Some tools become invisible when artists transmute them into formal compositions where the tool itself is without inherent significance. Iron fragments. Disconnected patterns. Remnants with facticity but without memory of time or place. Iron and wood artifacts laid aside, use unknown or forgotten, gone by, bent, broken. Artists transform the animism of orphan tools in compositions where the image of the tool itself becomes irrelevant.

In such work, the text is deleted, storytelling silenced, history-making obscured, the quenched and tempered tools now rusted relics. They are sledge-hammered icons from deconstructed reliquaries of art, lingering fragments of now unrecognizable history, born again in counterpoised compositions of ambiguity and harmony, old texts as new palimpsests.

The Art of Assemblage

A tiny slice of the plastic arts' pie, assemblage art explores the ironic relationship of finding versus making. Assemblage artists transfigure found objects, welding or crushing iron and steel tools into new compositions, rearranging wooden remnants or material culture detritus as reinvented parables in still life, collage, and improvised environments. Assemblage artists thus recapitulate the fundamental question about the work of that old revolutionary, Cézanne, i.e. what did he find (cones, cubes, and rectangles), and what did he make? The foundation of Modern Art was one hell of a construction.

Figure 45. H. G. Brack, *Dollar Whalebone*.

The arts of antiquity are replete with assemblages that still entice us. Bronze Age burials with chariots. Stone cairns in Brittany. Red paint scrapers at Wampanucket mortuary sites. Gargoyles as assembled images in Gothic architecture. The placement of everyday objects in Dutch interiors. Chardin's still lifes. Duchamp's ready-mades. Picasso's collages. Kurt Schwitter's orphaned ephemera. The twentieth century introduced atonal variations in the old melody of the assemblage of significant objects, a new iconography of insignificant objects, vehicles to ridicule received wisdom and journey into the surreal. Now modern artists await deconstruction by some new wave of twilight-zone iconoclasts slouching towards a post-apocalypse art historical Bethlehem.

And what of the finders who do not weld, hammer, or file, those who use juxtaposition to create evocative arrangements? They reanimate accidental durable remnants in unique combines. New texts arise out of the debris of deconstruction. Using hand, eye, and irony, artists rearrange found artifacts in new patterns of the familiar.

Technology and Conceptual Art

When the legacy of technology becomes the target of conceptual art, the text sometimes becomes unpalatable, annoying, anti-storytelling, or unfathomable. Should we plug off the tunnels to certain claustrophobic labyrinths of history when constructions and inscriptions tell us stories we would rather not read or hear, tales of the subterranean juxtaposition of archaic red paint scrapers and traveling plumes from the all-encompassing troposphere of Mr. Anomalous Electronic Voltage and his chlorinated, methylated siblings?

Cyberspace word sculptors scribble unwanted notations in our exploding electronic environs. Radnet Freedom of Information on Anthropogenic Radioactivity on the world wide web. Biosphere as bank account. Free trade in chemical fallout. Odes to the autistic. The cumulative fallout index. How many becquerels of radiocesium in your square meter? Time to split the firewood.

Figure 46. Donna Just, *Window Still Life*.

Convivial Interactive Art

And last, there is interactive art – a balloon-framed building filled with tools, hardware, found objects, books, iconography, the gestalt of the used hardware store, a late twentieth century happening. Enter. Remove tools and other objects of interest. Exit. Chisel the mortise. Repair the car. Take down the woodshed. Or create new images that reaffirm life's journey from artifact, history, lingering memory to epiphany, sanctuary, reliquary, and the poetry of beautiful objects.

What artifacts and tools can we salvage from that vast network of our cityscapes? Can we yet redecorate our lives with lost, then found, detritus from our abandoned suburban battlegrounds, resurrected icons that assert the necessity of retrieving in the age of the post-apocalypse?

Assembled environments of found objects and useful tools remind us that finders rewrite the text. They choose mundane function or create cozy combines or gorgeous art with accidental durable remnants, making do and making new, reinventing old artifacts in new arrangements that celebrate the marriage of tools, art, and history.

Phenomenology of Tools

The phenomenology of tools is the totality of the voices of tools in history, a large extended family of function, skill, technique, necessity, history, obsolescence, memory, expressed in a cacophony of images and artifacts, all squabbling to be used or laid aside, remembered or forgotten. From eolith to atomic bomb, from artisans to nation states, the craftsmanship and history making of tools join with the archaeology of tools to construct, deconstruct and again reconstruct the stories of history. The toolmaker and artist join in creative acts, the first pleasure of any text, which express the noumenal through the phenomenal. Or, in plain English, they create beautiful objects, images, and evocative arrangements. Iconographers or iconoclasts, artists take us on a journey into the labyrinths of artifact/art transfigurations and tool/icon transmigrations, i.e. the marriage of tools, art, and history. Let these journeys distract us from our daily routines and elicit in us new ways of seeing the world.

We thank the artists who participated in this show for taking us on such a journey.

Appendix A: Eaton's Boatyard

To make do, make a living:
                      to throw away nothing,
practically nothing, nothing that may
come in handy:
        within an inertia of caked paintcans,
frozen C-clamps, blown strips of tarp, and
pulling-boat molds,
              to be able to find,
for whatever it's worth,
                    what has to be there:
the requisite tool
              in this cultch there's no end to:
the drawshave buried in potwarp,
chain, and manila jib sheets,
                  or under the bench,
the piece that already may fit
                          the idea it begins
to shape up:
              not to be put off by split rudders,
stripped outboards, half
a gasket, and nailslick garboards:
                      to forget for good
all the old year's losses,
            save for
what needs to be retrieved:
                    a life given to
how today feels:
            to make of what's here
what has to be made
to make do.

"Eaton's Boatyard", from LIFELINES by Philip Booth, copyright (c) 1999 by Philip Booth. Used by permission of Viking Penguin, a division of Penguin Group (USA) Inc.

The interpretation of the interrelationship between tools, art, and history begins with Philip Booth's poem, which expresses the fundamental simplicity of tools as commonplace artifacts of our everyday material existence. This poem is the starting point for a philosophical and historical journey which goes far beyond the everyday simplicity of the tools in the museum exhibits or incorporated in the compositions on display. It is this journey into the language of tools – what we term the "phenomenology of tools" – which is central to the exploration of the interrelationship of tools, art, and history. As with any aesthetic experience, words, as in the curator's riff on the "The Marriage of Tools, Art, and History," are an inadequate medium for describing living history, art, or their interrelationship. We hope the art displayed in this exhibition will fill in part of this void.

Appendix B: Notes and Commentary on the Illustrations

Cover

Alan Magee, *Tryptic: Thingpoem, Inheritance, Helix*
Numerous examples of Alan's extraordinary depiction of tools, many purchased from the Liberty Tool Company, now reside at the Davistown Museum. This tapestry is the centerpiece of the ongoing exhibition in the Main Hall of the Davistown Museum by an American master of the art of illustrating the marriage of tools, art, and history, i.e. the phenomenology of tools. www.alanmagee.com.

Figure 1. Carol Hanson, *Yemaya*
Located in the Davistown Museum Hulls Cove Sculpture Garden, Carol Hanson's creation is a compelling example of the magnificent art that can be created with hand tools.

Figure 2. Sett Balise, *Main Hall*
This view of the main exhibition hall of the Davistown Museum captures the diversity of art and artifacts in the museum exhibition. Thousands of artisans and artists forged, painted, sculpted, printed, or assembled the wide diversity of objects that illustrate the marriage of tools, art, and history. Each object has its own unique story, significance, or history.

Figure 3. *Collection of Shells and Beads in a Dish*
This extraordinary assemblage of shell, wampum, and mineral beads, was retrieved from a cave in California early in the 20th century by an archaeologist whose identity has been lost. These accidental durable remnants last resided in the attic of a home in Cohasset, MA, hence their current designation as the Cohasset Hoard.

Figure 4. *Birmingham Smooth Plane*
One of the most sculptural creations of the classic period of American toolmaking, this malleable iron plane was manufactured by the Birmingham Plane Mfg. Co., Birmingham, CT, 1855 – 1890.

Figure 5. Toby Stewart, *Patina*
This is a color photograph of the doors of David McLaughlin's *Abandoned Workshop* in the Davistown Museum Hulls Cove Sculpture Garden. The doors were salvaged from an abandoned warehouse on the St. Georges River in Warren, Maine and are significant as being a surviving example of

"Indian doors" where the metal exterior was intended to deter Indian attacks. Though built after the end of the Indian Wars and the Treaty of Quebec (1763), the existence of these late 18th century doors expressed the continuing fear of Indian attacks by the early settlers of Warren. The doors are also significant in representing one of the first uses metal galvanizing technology, an unintended image that uncovers history.

Figure 6. David McLaughlin, *Used Glove Salesperson's Bicycle: Post Apocalypse Series Number 3*
One of five of David McLaughlin's *Post Apocalypse Series* sculptures; the other four are located at the museum's Hulls Cove Sculpture Garden and are accessible year round from dawn to dusk.

Figure 48. *Abandoned Workshop.*

Figure 47. *Virgin Birth.*

David was a meticulous ironmonger and a master of the weld. His recent death is a stark reminder of the fleeting nature of our presence and the transience of our deliberate durable creations.

Figure 49. *Totem.*   **Figure 50.** *Junk Collector's Tricycle.*

Figure 7. *Wampum*
Our collection of wampum is a reminder of the florescence of the Native American communities of New England who preceded European settlement.

Figure 8. *Moose Hide Scraper*
This moose hide scraper came from Unity, ME, c. 1972 and was a last minute addition to the purchase of a 90 year old carpenters' woodworking tool collection. This scraper, along with several other tools, had been dug up in his yard and may be a late archaic remnant of the indigenous inhabitants of central coastal Maine.

Figure 9. *Rattle*
This Native American rattle is from a Midwestern (probably Sioux) community and incorporates the iconography of a conquering culture as expressed in the handicrafts of an indigenous community. Who was the intended audience for this icon of turtle shell, leather, bone, glass bead, horsehair, metal, and feather?

Figure 10. *Apache Mortar and Pestle*
The Apache community was traditionally a nomadic hunting and gathering culture. This artifact may express the desperate efforts of the Apache community to adapt to the pressures resulting from the intrusion of a predatory cowboy/military/market economy with a last minute attempt at horticulture, before being driven off their temporarily settled homelands by a final diaspora.

Figure 11. *Monte Alban Funerary Vase*
This is an inscrutable prehistoric image of a burial offering from an important Mexican cultural community. Does the gaze of the deity express the power of nature as it becomes transmuted by an anthropogenic idol?

Figure 12. *Gutter Adz*
One of a number of natural steel tools in the museum's collection, this gutter adz was probably made by the direct process of smelting bog iron, which was then forged into a wrought iron tool with a steeled cutting edge.

Figure 13. Unknown artist, *Medieval City with Serfs*
This 16th century copper plate engraving is a moving rendition of a German landscape (Cologne?), which expresses the high Renaissance interrelationship of agrarian and urban environments with a hint of lingering Eleusinian mystery.

Figure 14. Kilroy, *Earth Reliquary*
The *Reliquary* includes Michael Waterman's *Crucifixion* (oil on canvas) and is a sacred space occupied by accidental durable remnants from both Native American and Western cultures.

Figure 15. *Millers Falls Mortising Drill*
Manufactured by the Millers Falls Company, this drill is one of many instruments of manual operation that are the legacy of the inventive designers of the classic period of American toolmaking.

Figure 16. *Blacksmith Double Calipers*
A forge-welded blacksmith tool used to manufacture the vehicles and machinery of the dawn of the American factory system of mass production.

Figure 17. Nate Nichols, *Bike with Riders*
Nate Nichols is a Waldoboro sculptor with a number of pieces in the museum collection. Perhaps his riders are early contestants in modern global consumer society's race to oblivion.

Figure 18. *Buff and Buff Surveying Transit*
This transit is one of the most precise measuring tools of the classic period of American toolmaking and an icon of our ability to deconstruct our landscapes into slivers and slabs of real estate.

Figure 19. Phil Barter, *Gas Tank*
This is one of two gas tanks commissioned by the Davistown Museum from Sullivan, ME, artist, Phil Barter. Numerous other Barter sculptures and paintings reside in the museum's permanent collection.
www.bartergallery.com.

Figure 20. Buddy Swenson, *American Portrait #6: In a Time of War*
This is a classic image by the Kennebunk, ME, iconoclast Buddy Swenson. A number of other examples of his oeuvre are located in the permanent collection or in the Maine Artists Guild Gallery complex in Liberty.

Figure 21. H. G. Brack, *Mixed Grill Number 4: Anthropogenic Radioactivity*
These are selected accidental durable remnants of a global/military/industrial consumer society that uses nuclear fission to heat water.

Figure 22. Lauren Fensterstock, *Cheeseburger w/ Sesame Seeds and Accidental Durable Remnants*
Organochlorines are only one group of thousands of anthropogenic ecotoxins now contaminating the atmospheric water cycle and destined to reside in the biotic media of all living organisms.

Figure 23. *Davis Level*
The Davis Level & Tool Co. (1875-1892), originally founded by Leonard L. Davis in Springfield, MA (1867-1875), manufactured some of the most exquisite hand tools in the brief reign of American industrial society.

Figure 24. Aaron Stephan, *Wrench*
This is a most clever interpretation of the phenomenology of tools. Stephan's paper *Wrench* has the following inscription: "This wrench, made completely from Immanuel Kant's *The Critique of Judgment*, was used in an attempt to fix my truck. This text is the heady, philosophical root of much twentieth century art. With an unwieldy precision Kant defines abstract concepts like beauty, the sublime, and good. The wrench draws this text out of the abstract and into the world of things. Here, it seems, text fails in its in-ability to function."

Figure 25. David McLaughlin, *Study for Welds*
David's *Study for Welds* was the first sculpture traded for tools and displayed in the old Geronimo Sculpture Garden, now the Davistown Museum Hulls Cove Sculpture Garden. This construction, made from the old boilers at David's Liberty cannery, expresses his meticulous craftsmanship as one of America's most important and unrecognized assemblage artists (d. 2010).

Figure 26. J. Wood, *Box Scraper under Glass*
What messages might be communicated by the prescient voices of the accidental durable remnants of industrial society?

Figure 27. Obadiah Buell, *Arch (reliquary for carriage-maker's plane)*
One of Obadiah's evocative stone reliquaries is occupied by an unidentified masterpiece of America's 19th century toolmaking community.

Figure 28. Melita Westerlund, *Balancing Act*
As are so many of her sculptures, Melita's *Balancing Act*, is a color field melody of epiphanies and incantations that transcend the rationalizations of left brain tool-wielding.

Figure 29. H. G. Brack, *Socratic Dog*
The *Socratic Dog* is an accidental durable remnant that once resided at the bottom of an old tool chest. What messages does he have to tell us at the dawn of the age of biocatastrophe?

Figure 30. George Daniell, *Georgia O'Keefe at Her Home in NM*
This is an exquisite photograph of an American master of the dance of art.

Figure 31. Dan Falt, *Attack Rabbit*
Dan's zoomorphic rabbit is ready for an attack on nature, or is he? Mr. Rabbit, do you suffer from an incipient autism spectrum disorder or are you abnormally normal?

Figure 32. Squidge Davis, *Night Holding the Moon*
Squidge Davis is an artist from Monroe, ME, whose *Night Holding the Moon* quietly embraces a world in turmoil and would be an appropriate presence in an Obadiah Buell reliquary, a silent listener to the confessions of round-world rapists.

Figure 33. Lewis Iselin, *Agony*
Iselin was a Camden area, Maine, artist. As with *St. Francis*, *Agony* was abandoned as an unwanted artifact before becoming an evocative presence at the Hulls Cove Sculpture Garden, especially on moonlit nights with snowy landscapes.

Figure 34. Don (Brother Hugh) Vanesse, *Massachusetts Prisons 200 Years Later*
Don Vanesse was once a counselor at the Walpole State Prison in Massachusetts. Don's rendition of the prison weapons he encountered was initially shown at the 1988 Whitney Museum Downtown Branch (former first precinct police station) prison show, *Realities and Representations*, "painting, sculpture, photographs, films, video, and poetry from and about prison". Don is currently a brother in residence at the Monastery of the Holy Spirit, Conyers, GA.

Figure 35. H. G. Brack, *Three Wise Men and Baby Jesus*
The *Three Wise Men* were salvaged out of a cellar in Brookline, MA, which contained the workshop of an MIT physicist, who made mockup models of multiple reentry atomic missile warheads. The *Baby Jesus* is the remnant of an old keg of rusty nails.

Figure 36. Unknown artist, *St. Francis*
St. Francis's silent voice echoes in the moonlit and moonless nights of an eerily quiet sculpture garden. He blesses each passerby on the ancient Breakneck Hollow Rd. which traverses from Hulls Cove to the now abandoned Native American shell heaps and summer camps of Northeast Harbor and Fernald Point.

Back Cover

A photograph of Liberty Tool Co. before the three wise men migrated to the Hulls Cove Sculpture Garden. The Liberty Tool Co. is an interactive sculpture where the participants remove tools and other accidental durable remnants giving voice to the marriage of tools, art, and history by repairing, cultivating, or constructing engines, artifacts, gardens, and environments in the true tradition of a convivial phenomenology of tools. May the joy of convivial tools overcome the legacy of human ecology and the emerging threat of biocatastrophe.

Appendix C: Pennywheel Press Publications
www.davistownmuseum.org/publications.html

- Volume 4: *Norumbega Reconsidered: Mawooshen and the Wawenoc Diaspora*

Hand Tools in History Publication Series

- Volume 6: *Steel- and Toolmaking Strategies and Techniques before 1870*
- Volume 7: *Art of the Edge Tool: The Ferrous Metallurgy of New England Shipsmiths and Toolmakers from the Construction of Maine's First Ship, the Pinnace Virginia (1607), to 1882*
- Volume 8: *The Classic Period of American Toolmaking, 1827-1930*
- Volume 9: *An Archaeology of Tools: A Catalog of the Tool Collection of the Davistown Museum*
- Volume 10: *Registry of Maine Toolmakers*
- Volume 11: *Handbook for Ironmongers: A Glossary of Ferrous Metallurgy Terms: A Voyage through the Labyrinth of Steel- and Toolmaking Strategies and Techniques 2000 BC to 1950*

Phenomenology of Biocatastrophe Publication Series

- Volume 1: *Essays on Biocatastrophe and the Collapse of Global Consumer Society*
- Volume 2: *Biocatastrophe Lexicon: An Epigrammatic Journey Through the Tragedy of our Round-World Commons*
- Volume 3: *Biocatastrophe: The Legacy of Human Ecology: Toxins, Health Effects, Links, Appendices, and Bibliographies*

Note: The volume sequence of the publication series is based on the organization of the Davistown Museum website. Several other volumes not listed here will be published in the future, are works in progress, or are available upon request.

www.ingramcontent.com/pod-product-compliance
Lightning Source LLC
Chambersburg PA
CBHW042013150426

43196CB00002B/27